ANIMALS WITH SUPERPOWERS!

INVISIBILITY!

WRITTEN BY EMILIE DUFRESNE
DESIGNED BY AMY LI

Published in 2022 by
KidHaven Publishing, an Imprint of Greenhaven Publishing, LLC
353 3rd Avenue
Suite 255
New York, NY 10010

Edited by: Madeline Tyler
Designed by: Amy Li

Find us on

Cataloging-in-Publication Data

Names: Dufresne, Emilie.
Title: Invisibility! / Emilie Dufresne.
Description: New York : KidHaven Publishing, 2022. | Series: Animals with superpowers! | Includes glossary and index.
Identifiers: ISBN 9781534534933 (pbk.) | ISBN 9781534534957 (library bound) | ISBN 9781534534940 (6 pack) | ISBN 9781534534964 (ebook)
Subjects: LCSH: Camouflage (Biology)--Juvenile literature. | Protective coloration (Biology)--Juvenile literature. | Animals--Color--Juvenile literature. | Animal defenses--Juvenile literature.
Classification: LCC QL767.D847 2022 | DDC 591.47'2--dc23

Printed in the United States of America

CPSIA compliance information: Batch #CS22KH: For further information contact Greenhaven Publishing LLC, New York, New York at 1-844-317-7404.

Please visit our website, www.greenhavenpublishing.com. For a free color catalog of all our high-quality books, call toll free 1-844-317-7404 or fax 1-844-317-7405.

PHOTO CREDITS ***All images courtesy of Shutterstock. With thanks to Getty Images, Thinkstock Photo, and iStockphoto.***

Cover – Azamatovic, Lazerko A, UltraViolet, Zorana Matijasevic, Tiny Doz. Vector Animals – natchapohn, Andrew Rybalko (Professor Ax), Guz Anna (lion, sloth, frog, jellyfish), Mckenna71 (crab), natchapohn (moth), StockSmartStart (bear). Master images – TinyDoz (header font), Azamatovic, Natalisa (main and panel backgrounds), Zorana Matijasevic, UltraViolet (Comic bubbles, assets and annotations), Nata Alhontess (Speech bubbles and boxes), Lazerko A (page number cloud, stars). 1 – Lazerko A, 2-3 – Nata Alhontess, 4-5 – james weston, 6-7 – Targn Pleiades, Chris Fourie, enjoy your life, A78805, 8-9– Mark Brandon, robuart, Ravennka, Dusida, 10-11– Lorelyn Medina, Antonsov85, Eric Isslee, 12-13– Krushevskaya, Eric Isslee, Chinch, StockSmartStart, Festa, 14-15– Anna Frajtova, IanRedding, PinkPueblo, Meilun, 16-17– angkrit, Erin Donalson, PinkPueblo, Africa Studio, kungverylucky, 18-19– Baksiabat, Nadzin, THAIFINN, 20-21– DRogatnev, worldswildlifewonders, Dr Morley Read, imaginasty, 22-23– james weston, mhatzapa.

CONTENTS

Words that look like **this** can be found in the glossary on page 24.

SUPERHEROES
OF THE
FUTURE
The world is constantly in danger. Whether it's from crime, alien invasions, or humans destroying the planet, one thing is known for certain. Something has got to change...

A new generation of superheroes is needed to protect the planet.
Join me, Professor Ax, as I search high and low for the superheroes of the future. There's no time to lose – let's get started!

INVISIBILITY

This could be through camouflage...

...or by being transparent.

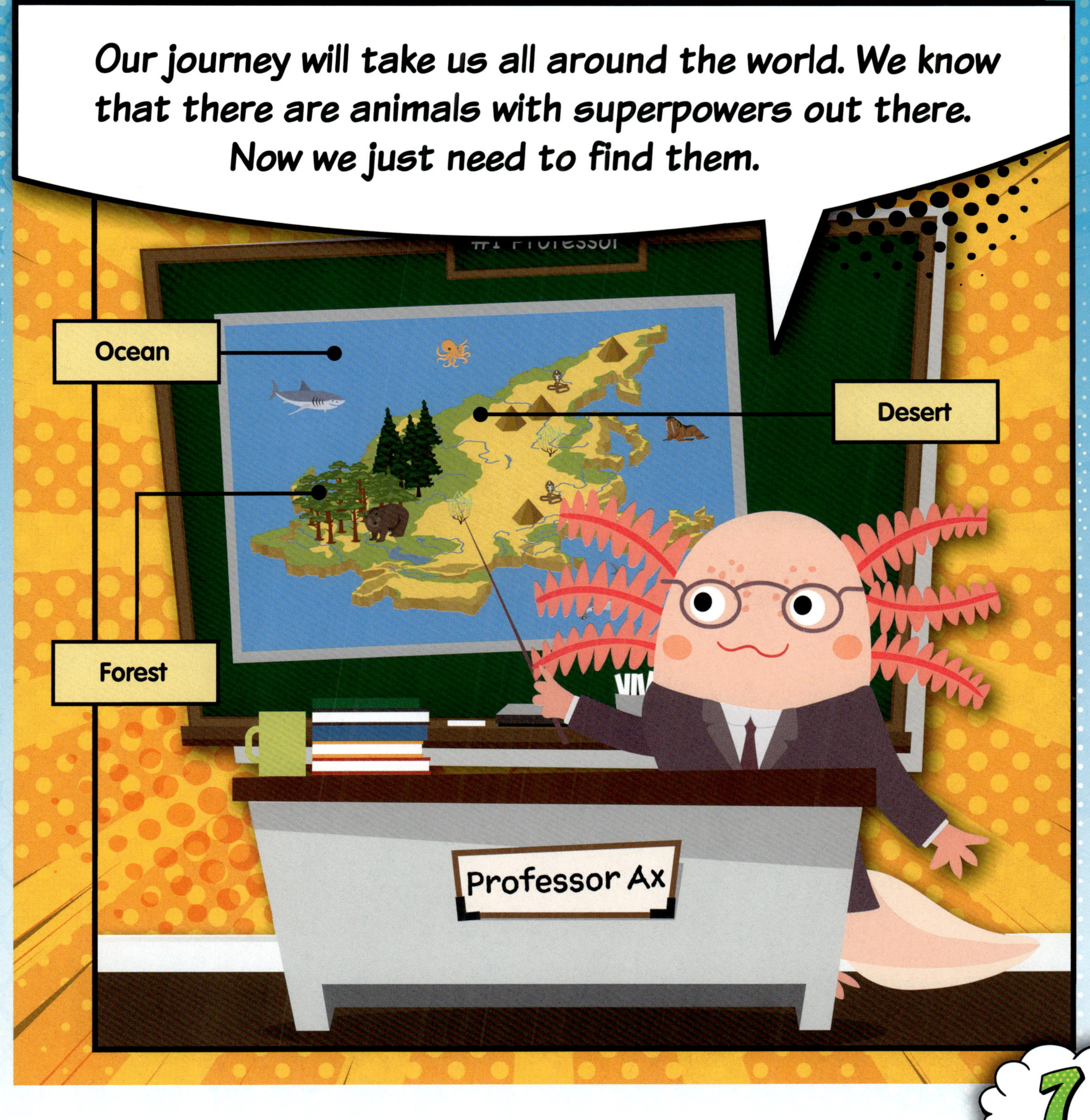
Our journey will take us all around the world. We know that there are animals with superpowers out there. Now we just need to find them.
Ocean
Desert
Forest
Professor Ax

HERMIT CRABS

Hermit crabs find shells to use to protect their soft abdomens. These shells also come in handy when they need to hide from predators.

The crab can hide completely inside its shell!

Is it safe to come out yet?

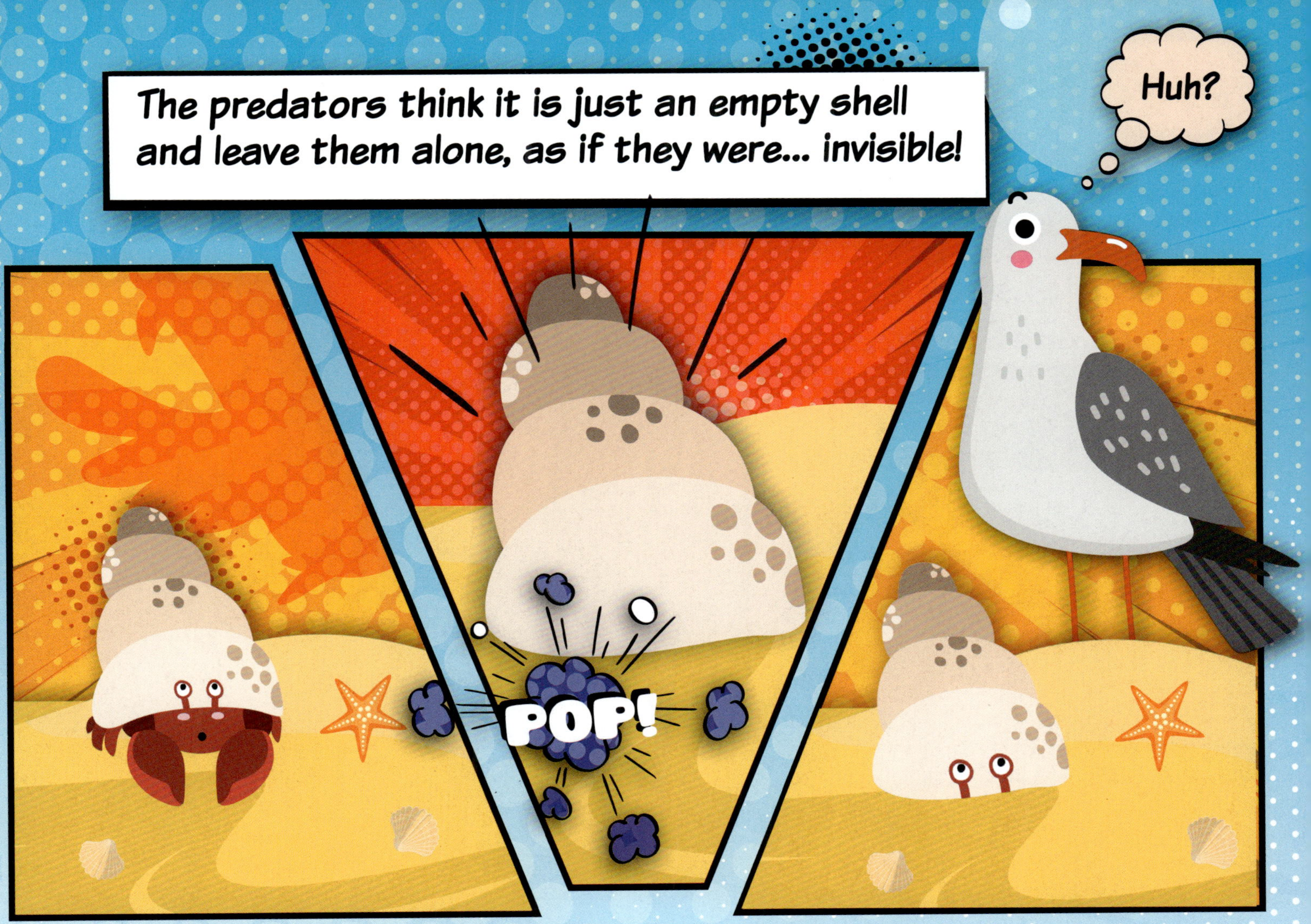

The predators think it is just an empty shell and leave them alone, as if they were... invisible!

POP!

Huh?

NAME:	Hermit crab
LIVES:	In the sea or on land, inside shells
SIZE:	Up to 7.9 inches (20 cm)
SUPERPOWER:	Can hide its whole body in its shell whenever needed

Lions are very good at following and hunting their prey. They camouflage themselves in the grass and then jump out on their prey.

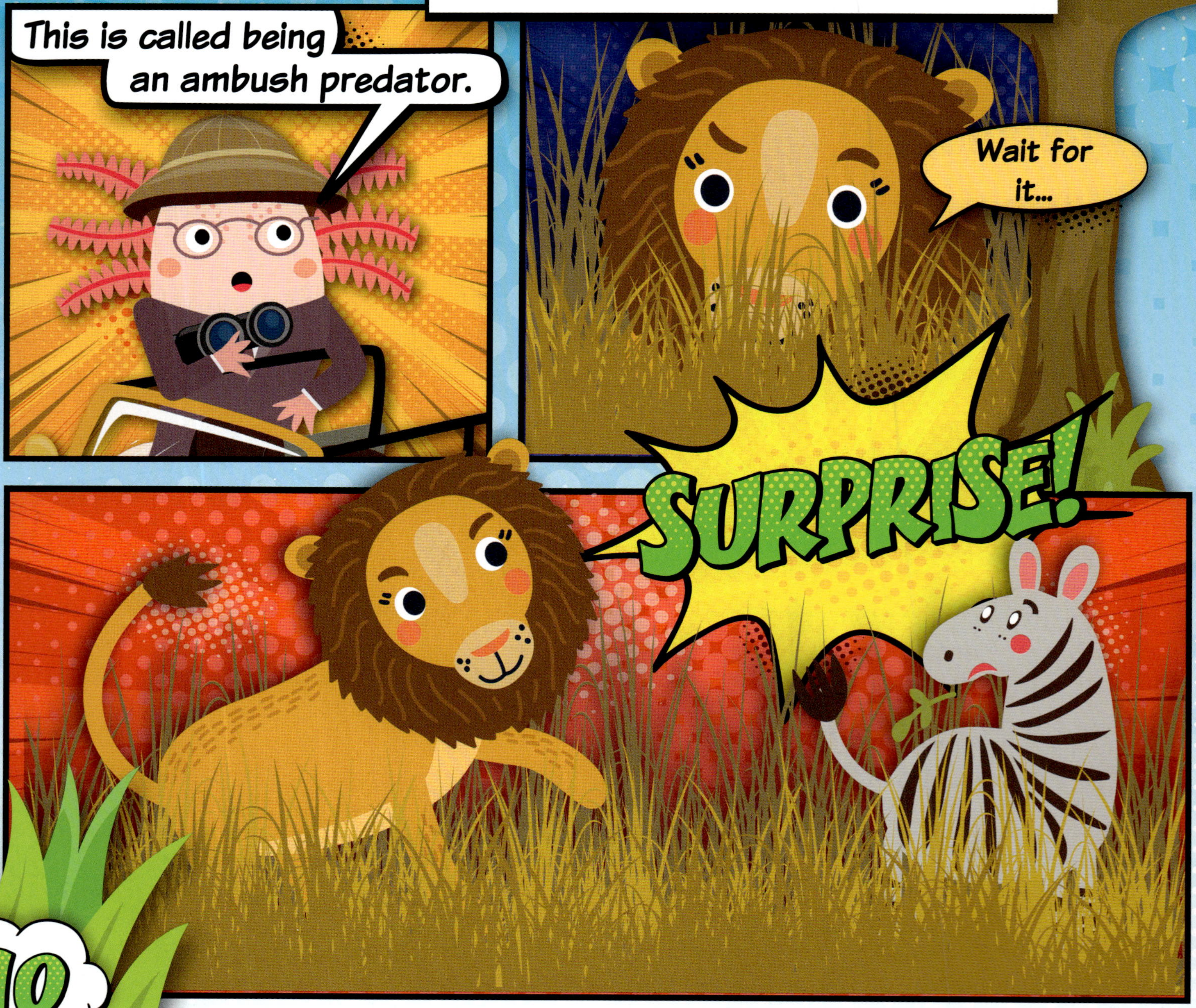

Their sandy-colored fur helps them to blend in with the dry, arid conditions that they live in.
Sand-Colored Camouflaged Fur
ROARRRR!
FACT FILE
NAME: Lion
LIVES: Sub-Saharan Africa and Asia
SIZE: Up to 6.6 feet (2 m) long
SUPERPOWER: Camouflaged ambush predator
11

POLAR BEARS

Polar Bear Fur

This makes them one of the hardest animals to spot in the wild.

FACT FILE

NAME: Polar bear

LIVES: On Arctic ice sheets

SIZE: Over 6.6 feet (2 m) tall

SUPERPOWER: See-through fur that camouflages their bodies

PEPPERED MOTHS

This makes it harder for predators to see them.

Hoo dear. There's no food anywhere.

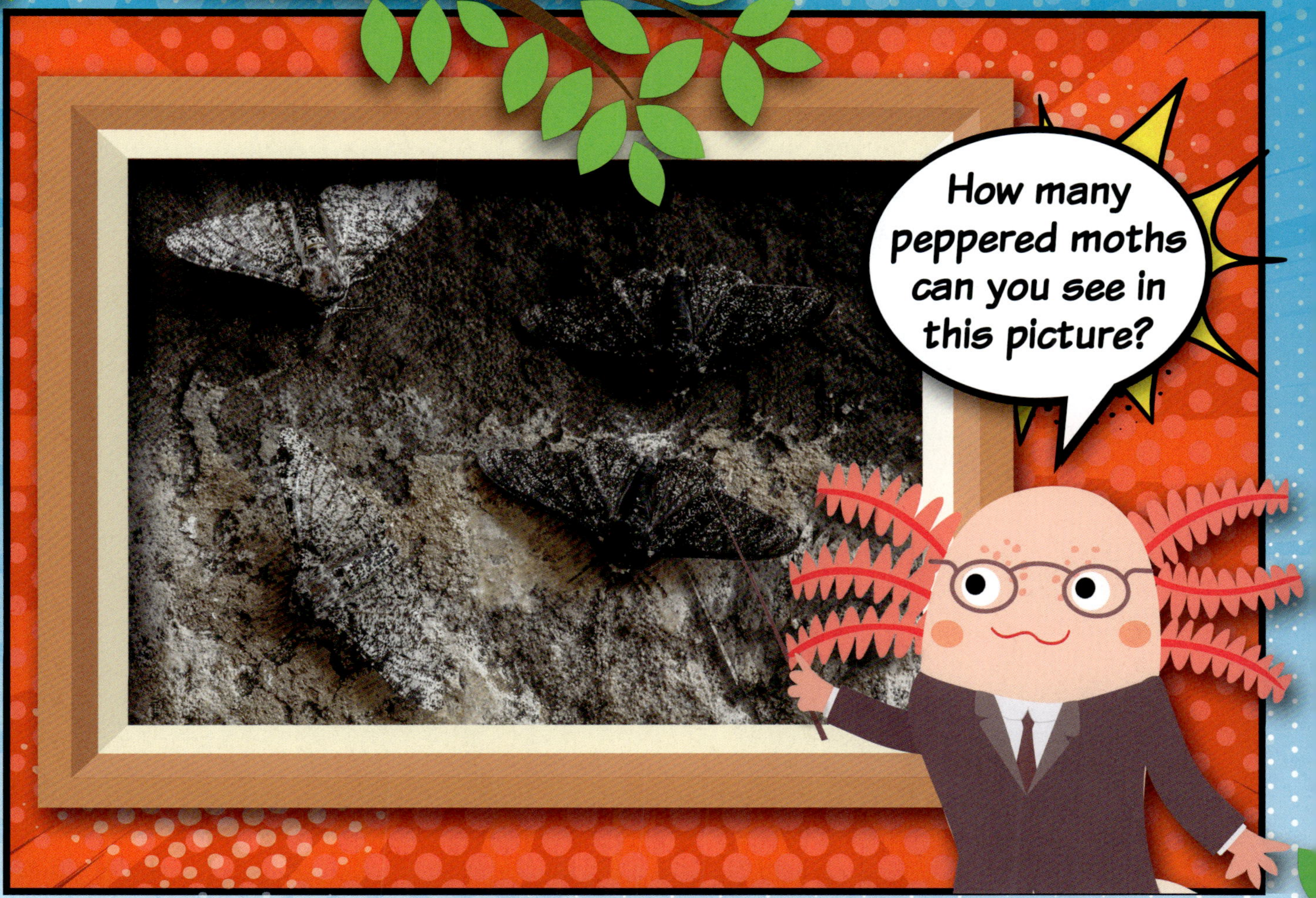

NAME: Peppered moth

LIVES: Europe, North America, and Asia

SIZE: A wingspan of around 2.4 inches (6 cm)

SUPERPOWER: Hides in plain sight using its patterned wings

SLOTHS

Sloths spend most of their time in trees. They often go unseen by predators because of how slowly they move.

They can move so slowly that algae can grow on them. This also adds extra camouflage.

Oh good – a new patch of algae!

Algae on a Sloth's Fur

FACT FILE

NAME:	Sloth
LIVES:	Central and South America
SIZE:	Up to 23.6 inches (60 cm) long
SUPERPOWER:	Being so slow, they are barely even noticed

CRYSTAL JELLY

If these jellyfish are disturbed, they do something extraordinary...

FACT FILE

NAME: Crystal jelly

LIVES: Coastal areas near the Pacific Ocean

SIZE: **Bell** up to 9.8 inches (25 cm) in **diameter**

SUPERPOWER: Transparent unless disturbed

GLASS FROGS

The glass frog has a transparent underside to its body.

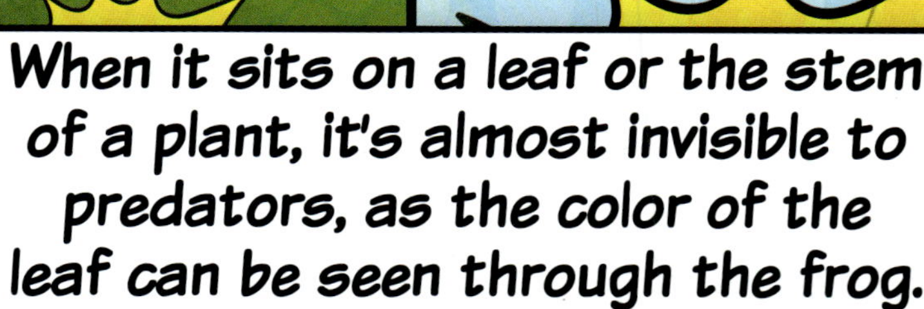

I'm the top frog at hide-and-seek!

The glass frog is so transparent that you can see through to its organs!

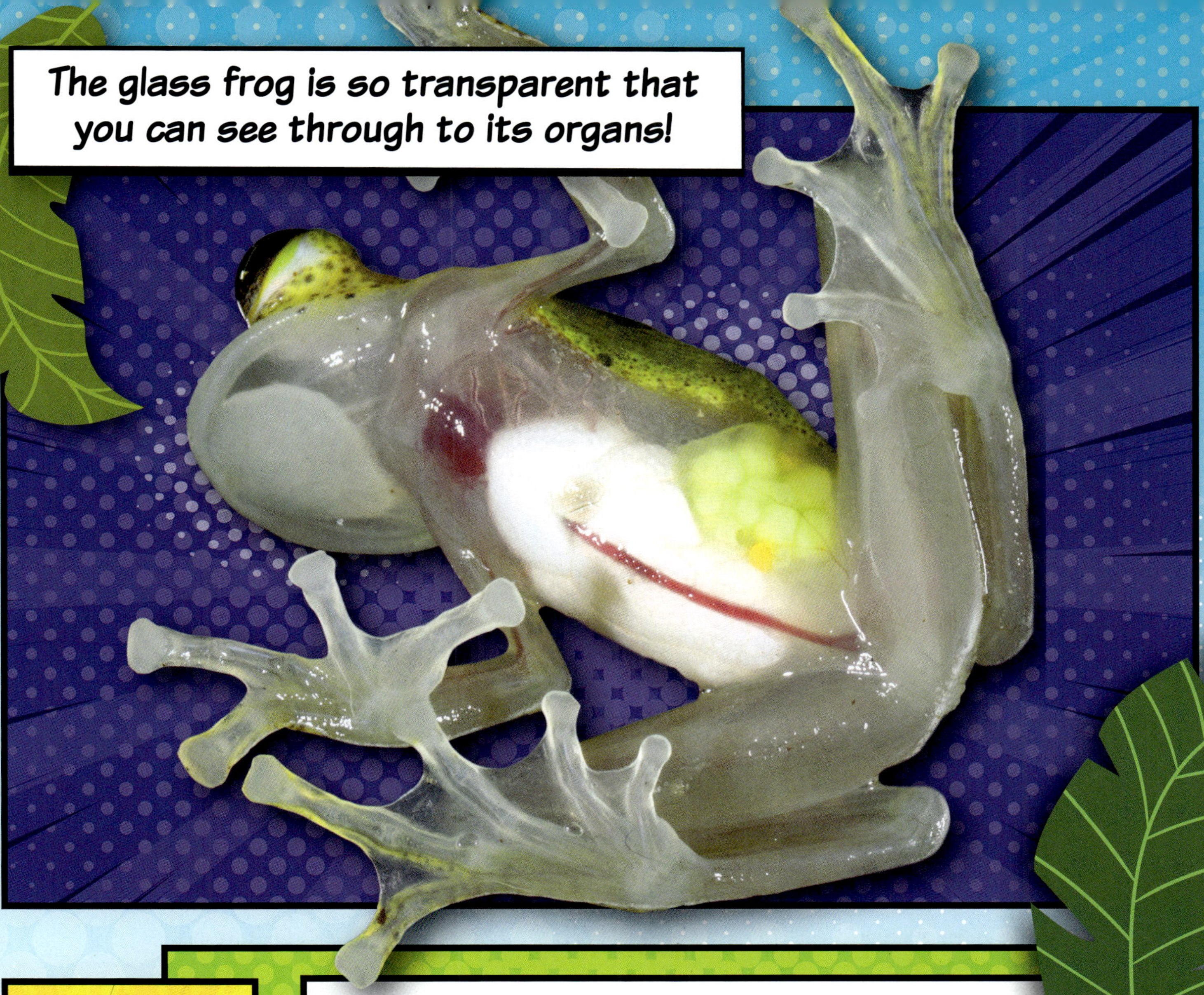

FACT FILE

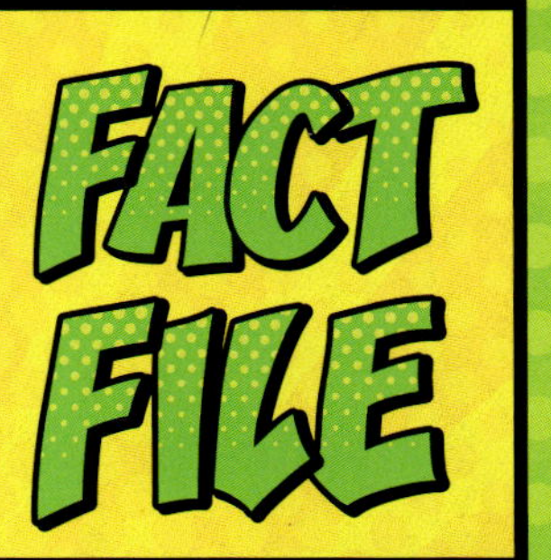

NAME:	Glass frog
LIVES:	Central and South American rain forests
SIZE:	Up to 3.1 inches (8 cm) long
SUPERPOWER:	See-through body camouflages on any leaf

THE NEXT GENERATION

THE HIDDEN WING

CAMO - FROGGED

LION-IN-WAIT

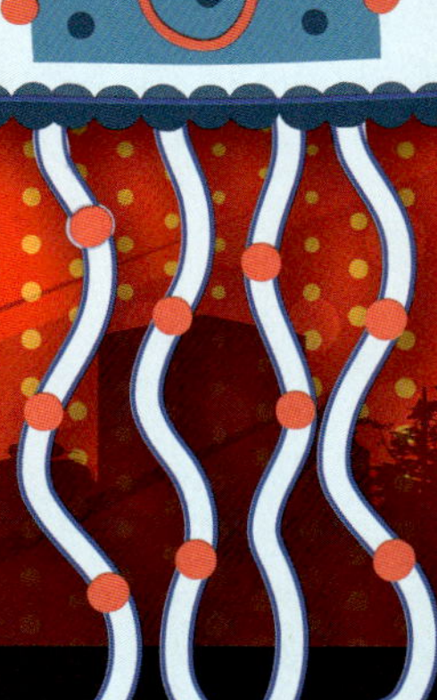

HIDE AND SWIM

ARE YOU AN INVISIBILITY SUPERHERO?

Why not have a game of hide-and-seek in your house? Where would be best to hide? What clothes could you wear so that people won't notice you as easily?

GLOSSARY

abdomens the parts of bodies that are between the hips and chest

algae a plant or plantlike living thing that has no roots, stems, leaves, or flowers

arid describing an area of dry land without much rain that can't support many plants

bell the round "head" part of a jellyfish

camouflage traits that allow an animal to hide itself in a habitat

diameter the distance through the center of an object

generation a group of people that have a similar age or are involved in a particular activity

insulated able to keep warmth inside of something

predators animals that hunt other animals for food

prey animals that are eaten for food

reflect to bounce back light, heat, or sound

transparent describing a material that lets light pass through it, causing it to be see-through

INDEX